REFLECTIONS
of

The Sea

COMPILED BY JOHN HADFIELD

PICTURES FROM THE TATE GALLERY

A GRAHAM TARRANT BOOK

DAVID & CHARLES
Newton Abbot · London · North Pomfret (Vt)

Designed by Julia Alldridge Associates
Cover paper design by courtesy of the Italian Paper Shop, London

British Library Cataloguing in Publication Data

Reflections of the sea.—(A Graham Tarrant book)
 1. English literature 2. Ocean—Literary
collections
 I. Hadfield, John, *1907–*   II. Tate Gallery
820.8′032162   PR1111.02/

ISBN 0-7153-8854-1

Typeset by Typesetters (Birmingham) Ltd,
Smethwick, West Midlands
and printed in The Netherlands
by Royal Smeets Offset, Weert
for David & Charles Publishers plc
Brunel House   Newton Abbot   Devon

Published in the United States of America
by David & Charles Inc
North Pomfret   Vermont 05053   USA

Day!
Faster and more fast,
O'er night's brim, day boils at last;
Boils, pure gold, o'er the cloud-cup's brim
Where spurting and suppressed it lay,
For not a froth-flake touched the rim
Of yonder gap in the solid gray
Of the eastern cloud, an hour away;
But forth one wavelet, then another, curled,
Till the whole sunrise, not to be suppressed,
Rose, reddened, and its seething breast
Flickered in bounds, grew gold, then overflowed the world.

ROBERT BROWNING
'Pippa Passes', *Bells and Pomegranates*, 1841

J M W TURNER
Yacht approaching the Coast, c 1835–40

Is she not beautiful? reposing there
    On her own shadow, with her white wings furled;
Moveless, as in the sleepy sunny air,
    Rests the meek swan in her own quiet world.

Is she not beautiful? her graceful bow
    Triumphant rising o'er th' enamour'd tides
That, glittering in the noon-day sunbeam, now
    Just leap and die along her polished sides.

NOEL THOMAS CARRINGTON
My Native Village and Other Poems, 1830

CHARLES BROOKING (1723–59)
A Flagship before the Wind (detail)

To sea! To sea! The calm is o'er;
The wanton water leaps in sport,
And rattles down the pebbly shore;
The dolphin wheels, the sea-cows snort,
And unseen Mermaids' pearly song
Comes bubbling up, the weeds among.
    Fling broad the sail, dip deep the oar:
To sea! To sea! The calm is o'er.
To sea! To sea! Our wide-winged bark
Shall billowy cleave its sunny way,
And with its shadow, fleet and dark,
Break the caved Tritons' azure ray,
Like mighty eagle soaring light
O'er antelopes on Alpine height.
    The anchor heaves, the ship swings free,
The sails swell full: To sea! To sea!

THOMAS LOVELL BEDDOES
Death's Jest-Book, 1850

ALFRED WALLIS
Schooner under the Moon, c 1935–6

THE first glimpse you get of Cowes, from the Southampton ferry, is of cranes and a tall factory chimney. But you look again, and the background has become trees and gentle hills and Victorian villas, and there in the foreground – at Regatta time anyway – the crowds of little boats, gay as gardenias, with glossy hulls and bright bunting, and the sails of those already astir as white as soap-flake advertisements in the innocent morning sunshine, all as saucy as a Dufy.

I arrived on the first early-morning ferry-boat, sailing down Southampton Water in a heavy aroma of breakfast, as though the crew were shovelling bacon and eggs into the boilers. The sky was a blaze of blue at eight o'clock; every craft was dressed overall for the town's own special day of the week's Regatta, from the Royal Yacht and the British, French, and Ecuadorian warships – very modest warships, all of them – down to the smallest vessels capable of carrying flags or bunting or pennants. The moored boats were ranged as neatly side by side as guardsmen, and as brightly dressed, and the wash from our self-important little steamer set their tall spars swinging like metronomes.

There is nothing breakneck about this kind of racing. At various times throughout the morning, hoarse little gunshots from the Royal Yacht Squadron's battery send yachts of all kinds of colour and size wheeling like lazy birds, dipping and rearing like the gentlest of rocking horses, around the marking-buoys and across the middle distance.

CYRIL RAY
Merry England, 1960

PHILIP WILSON STEER
A Procession of Yachts, 1892–3

THERE is no piece of inland water in the world so crowded . . . as this three-spoked lake of the Solent, Spithead and Southampton Water. There is none upon which so many thousands for a lifetime past have spent their leisure, and none which is thought to be more exhausted in all that can be known of it. But those who think so, neglect the dimension of time. For, though you should know every entry and every sounding, the first hour in every flood when your craft can safely go over the banks, the dredged channel under the Hampshire coast, and Lymington River, and Cowes Roads and Ryde Sands, and Beaulieu and Buckier's Hard, where I am told they launched great men of war, and Portsmouth Harbour right up to Fareham, and the Hamble to its bridge, and all the yard and wharfs of the Test and the Itchen, yet you do not possess that piece of water unless you see moving upon it the fulness of its past.

You must see the last tragedy of the Civil Wars: the craft that might have taken Charles away from Southampton to freedom, and his young son cruising with the loyal fleet (which had declared for the King against the oligarchy), cruising just outside the Wight, but unable to save the King at Carisbrooke . . . You must see the pirate boats of a thousand years ago stranded on the Bramble, because they did not know the water, and Alfred's men capturing them so, and taking them off to Chichester to be hanged: a proper end for all Vikings. And you must see the great fleet of Roman transports coming in by an August night with a comet in the sky, for the recovery of Britain seceded and turned into a separate realm; the German mercenaries landing and pouring up the Winchester road, and meeting their fellow-Germans in battle before London, and the Emperor Theodosius riding up Ludgate Hill in triumph after the usurper's death.

HILAIRE BELLOC
The Cruise of the Nona, 1925

J M W TURNER
*Spithead: Two Captured Danish Ships entering
Portsmouth Harbour*, 1807–9 (detail)

The sea is calm to-night,
The tide is full, the moon lies fair
Upon the Straits; – on the French coast the light
Gleams, and is gone; the cliffs of England stand,
Glimmering and vast, out in the tranquil bay.
Come to the window, sweet is the night-air!
Only, from the long line of spray
Where the ebb meets the moon-blanch'd land,
Listen! you hear the grating roar
Of pebbles which the waves suck back, and fling,
At their return, up the high strand,
Begin, and cease, and then again begin,
With tremulous cadence slow, and bring
The eternal note of sadness in.

MATTHEW ARNOLD
'Dover Beach', *New Poems*, 1867

GRAHAM BELL
Dover Front, 1938

THE Pool of London is fascinating always – untidy, disorderly, grim, ugly, beautiful, dramatic; not dramatic with the nonsense of detective fiction, but in the true sense of things being done – things primitive, interesting and important. The sedulous, swift tugs (that never make a mistake) fuss in and out about the 'roads' and wharves with their long trails of heavy lighters, as easily as a great lady whisking her train about a diplomatic ball-room. Ships lie loading or unloading under the tall cranes, or, safe in dock, thrust up their masts and funnels above the warehouses, and seem, from the river, to be floating in the streets . . . Ships, at high-water time, nosing their way in and out of the docks; little ships disappearing into secret alley-ways, like rabbits going to ground, or steaming haughtily away down-river, as if they were the *Mauretania*. A lonely lighterman, late for his tide, and with two great sweeps toilsomely urging his unwieldy craft upon the ever-slackening tide, fearful that the ebb may catch him short of his destination . . .

And in the evening, a little after sunset, you may enjoy what I judge to be the most lovely experience in London – the journey through the dusk from Wapping to Westminster. There are not many lights in the Pool; the warehouses are dark, become dignified and mysterious, palaces, fortresses, or temples . . . The starboard light of a steamer coming up on the flood round the bend astern of you is a brilliant emerald, the eye of some pursuing monster; she sends her final hoot of warning to the Tower Bridge, the thrilling announcement that another ship has come home; the Tower Bridge is a colourless outline, a children's toy, against the faint rose of the western sky, and St. Paul's dome, beyond, is only the ghost of a dome.

SIR ALAN HERBERT
No Boats on the River, 1932

ANDRE DERAIN
The Pool of London, 1906

All where the eye delights, yet dreads to roam,
The breaking billows cast the flying foam
Upon the billows rising – all the deep
Is restless change; the waves so swell'd and steep,
Breaking and sinking, and the sunken swells,
Nor one, one moment, in its station dwells:
But nearer land you may the billows trace,
As if contending in their watery chase;
May watch the mightiest till the shoal they reach,
Then break and hurry to their utmost stretch;
Curl'd as they come, they strike with furious force,
And then re-flowing, take their grating course,
Raking the rounded flints, which ages past
Roll'd by their rage, and shall to ages last.

GEORGE CRABBE
The Borough, 1810

THOMAS CHURCHYARD (1798–1865)
Aldeburgh Beach

The rushes blink in quaint surprise,
Wave-startled with a thousand eyes,
And merry blossoms from the grass
Twinkle good morrow as we pass.
Swift down the stream! The silver streak
Curls whispering from the glowing cheek:
O'er curving arm a crystal shower
Crowns the smooth rush of conscious power.
Strong speeds the stroke . . . In light new born
We leap to catch the kiss of morn:
New hopes salute a summer day.
New winds of thought shrill gladly by;
Gone is the night and the dusk of showers;
Beauty's awake, and the day is ours!

GEOFFREY WINTHROP YOUNG
'A morning bathe', *Wind and Hill*, 1909

HENRY SCOTT TUKE
August Blue, 1893

THERE are few things in this world that produce a greater sense of satisfaction than to sail your own boat across the sea and into a foreign port. She may be only ten tons, but you have most of the rights – as well as the responsibilities – inherent in captaining the largest ship afloat, including (bureaucracy be praised!) the right to take on tobacco and liquor 'out of bond,' in other words free of Customs Duty . . .

Why do people do it? It's not just to get to the other side, the way the mountaineer thinks of getting to the top. And this sort of day and night sailing in dangerous waters is far removed from just 'messing about in boats.' My own feeling is that it is a combination of many things – the challenge, the exhilaration of using, and sometimes fighting, the elements, the sense of achievement when you have made your landfall and brought your boat safe into a foreign port . . .

And around you, your few chosen companions; tired maybe, but content, making light of the little nuisances – the drip that has developed from the deck roof, the pump in the heads (the lavatory) that has jammed and must be cleared – reverting to a boyhood level of humour because they are relaxed and at peace with the world . . .

And most important of all, there is the ship herself. Her wooden hull is like a violin, magnifying every sound – and she talks as she ploughs through the waves. There is a little gremlin lives in a working beam above my bunk, and in heavy weather I have heard it whispering to me in a creaking voice, 'Too much sail – too much sail.' And in quieter conditions it chatters gaily. 'Getting along fine now, getting along fine . . .'

HAMMOND INNES
Harvest of Journeys, 1960

RAOUL DUFY
Deauville, Drying the Sails, 1933 (detail)

Sudden from the hills,
O'er rocks and woods, in broad brown cataracts,
A thousand snow-fed torrents shoot at once;
And, where they rush, the wide-resounding plain
Is left one slimy waste. Those sullen seas,
That wash'd th' ungenial Pole, will rest no more
Beneath the shackles of the mighty North,
But, rousing all their waves, resistless heave.
And, hark! the lengthening roar continuous runs
Athwart the rifted deep: at once it bursts,
And piles a thousand mountains to the clouds.
Ill fares the bark, with trembling wretches charged,
That, toss'd amid the floating fragments, moors
Beneath the shelter of an icy isle,
While night o'erwhelms the sea, and horrid looks
More horrible. Can human force endure
Th' assembled mischiefs that besiege them round? –
Heart-gnawing hunger, fainting weariness,
The roar of winds and waves, the crush of ice,
Now ceasing, now renew'd with louder rage,
And in dire echoes bellowing round the main,
More to embroil the deep, Leviathan
And his unwieldy train, in dreadful sport,
Tempest the loosen'd brine; while through the gloom,
Far from the bleak inhospitable shore,
Loading the winds, is heard the hungry howl
Of famish'd monsters, there awaiting wrecks . . .

JAMES THOMSON
The Seasons, 1726

J M W TURNER
Snow Storm: Steam-Boat off a Harbour's Mouth, 1842

Who told thee that the scenes of other lands
Were far more beautiful than aught in mine?
Who told thee that the soothing sounds of song
Fell on the ear from classic fields afar
More musical than down our thymy braes?
Who told thee that the Alps and Apennines
Had more of wildness in their very names
Than all the wonders of our Cornish coast?
Ramble among our valleys, climb our hills,
Gaze on our bulwarks red at setting sun,
Mark well our bays strewn with the whitest sand,
Muse on our moors, and wonder in our mines;
Linger among our ivy-cover'd walls;
List the sweet breezes playing through the ferns,
Where sings the robin, and o'erhead the lark;

Stand by our castles and our monuments,
Our towns and hamlets and religious fanes;
And look upon the dark-green rocks that lie
Beneath the Atlantic surges, or on those
That tower on high in awful craggy peaks,
Rolling eternal diapasons wild
To the great billows' bass; and when within
The pillar'd grotto of the famed Land's End,
Bethink thee of the scenes of other shores,
And let thy heart be friendly to mine own.

JOHN HARRIS (1820–84)
'The Land's End'

OSCAR KOKOSCHKA
Polperro II, 1939

I REMEMBER the smell of sea and seaweed, wet flesh, wet hair, wet bathing-dresses, the warm smell as of a rabbity field after rain, the smell of pop and splashed sunshades and toffee, the stable-and-straw smell of hot, tossed, tumbled, dug, and trodden sand, the swill-and-gaslamp smell of Saturday night, though the sun shone strong, from the bellying beer-tents, the smell of the vinegar on shelled cockles, winkle-smell, shrimp-smell, the dripping-oily backstreet winter-smell of chips in newspapers, the smell of ships from the sun-dazed docks round the corner of the sand-hills, the smell of the known and paddled-in sea moving, full of the drowned and herrings, out and away and beyond and further still towards the antipodes that hung their koala-bears and Maoris, kangaroos, and boomerangs, upside down over the backs of the stars.

And the noise of pummelling Punch, and Judy falling, and a clock tolling or telling no time in the tenantless town; now and again a bell from a lost tower or a train on the lines behind us clearing its throat, and always the hopeless, ravenous swearing and pleading of the gulls, donkey-bray and hawker-cry, harmonicas and toy trumpets, shouting and laughing and singing, hooting of tugs and tramps, the clip of the chair-attendant's puncher, the motor-boat coughing in the bay, and the same hymn and washing of the sea that was heard in the Bible.

DYLAN THOMAS
'Holiday Memory', *Quite Early One Morning*, 1954

CHARLES CUNDALL
Bank Holiday, Brighton, 1933 (detail)

For how long known this boundless wash of light,
  This smell of purity, this gleaming waste,
This wind? This brown, strewn wrack how old a sight,
  These pebbles round to touch and salt to taste.

See, the slow marbled heave, the liquid arch,
  Before the waves' procession to the land
Flowers in foam; the ripples' onward march,
  Their last caresses on the pure hard sand.

For how long known these bleaching corks, new-made
  Smooth and enchanted from the lapping sea?
Since first I laboured with a wooden spade
  Against this background of Eternity.

FRANCES CORNFORD
'Summer Beach', *Travelling Home*, 1948

PHILIP WILSON STEER
The Beach at Walberswick, 1889

WE ARE among the olive-coated stones at the verge of the far-receded tide, among which the springs from the cliffs, having broken out from various points in the shingle beach, are making for themselves tortuous channels on their way to the deserting sea. Their water, originally fresh, of course, has, by the time it arrives here, become so brackish by washing the salt stones and sea-weeds that the sand-hoppers and worms which inhabit the hollows under the stones are bathed in it with impunity . . . Great tufts of bladder wrack and other *Fuci* spring from the lower stones, and now lie flaccid about, awaiting the returning tide to erect them and wave their leathery leaves to and fro. Broad fronds of *Ulva*, too, like tissue paper of the tenderest green, irregularly crumpled and waved and nibbled and gnawed into thousands of holes, lie crisp and tempting; and tufts of a darker, duller green, and others of purple brown, and others again of rosy crimson, stud these rough stones and vary their ruggedness with elegance and beauty; a beauty, however, far more appreciable if we could look upon it when the flowing tide creeps up, with its calm water clear as crystal, and covers the many-hued parterre, softening and displaying the graceful outlines and the brilliant colours. Then, too, tiny creatures would be seen agilely swimming from weed to weed, or lithely twining among the fronds.

PHILIP HENRY GOSSE, FRS
A Year at the Shore, 1865

WILLIAM DYCE
Pegwell Bay, Kent. A Recollection of October 5, 1858, 1859–60

THE tremulous sea itself, when I could find sufficient pause to look at it, in the agitation of the blinding wind, the flying stones and sand, and the awful noise, confounded me. As the high watery walls came rolling in, and, at their highest, tumbled into surf, they looked as if the least would engulf the town. As the receding wave swept back with a hoarse roar, it seemed to scoop out deep caves in the beach, as if its purpose were to undermine the earth. When some white-headed billows thundered on, and dashed themselves to pieces before they reached the land, every fragment of the late whole seemed possessed by the full might of its wrath, rushing to be gathered to the composition of another monster. Undulating hills were changed to valleys, undulating valleys (with a solitary storm-bird sometimes skimming through them) were lifted up to hills; masses of water shivered and shook the beach with a booming sound; every shape tumultuously rolled on, as soon as made, to change its shape and place, and beat another shape and place away; the ideal shore on the horizon, with its towers and buildings, rose and fell; the clouds flew fast and thick; I seemed to see a rending and upheaving of all nature.

CHARLES DICKENS
David Copperfield, 1849

J M W TURNER
Waves breaking on a Lee Shore, c 1835

There was not, on that day, a speck to stain
The azure heaven; the blessed Sun alone,
In unapproachable divinity,
Careered, rejoicing in his fields of light.
How beautiful, beneath the bright-blue sky,
The billows heave! one glowing green expanse,
Save where along the bending line of shore
Such hue is thrown as when the peacock's neck
Assumes its proudest tint of amethyst,
Imbathed in emerald glory . . .
It was a day that sent into the heart
A summer feeling . . . the Rocks and Shores,
The Forest, and the everlasting Hills,
Smiled in that joyful sunshine, – they partook
The universal blessing . . .

ROBERT SOUTHEY
Madoc, 1835

JAMES ABBOT MCNEILL WHISTLER
Crepuscule in Flesh Colour and Green: Valparaiso, 1866

Mr and Mrs Stephen Grosvenor-Smith
(He manages a Bank in Nottingham)
Have come to Sandy Cove for thirty years
And now they think the place is going down.
'Not what it was, I'm very much afraid.
Look at that little mite with *Attaboy*
Printed across her paper sailor hat.
Disgusting, isn't it? Who *can* they be,
Her parents, to allow such forwardness?'
   The Browns, who thus are commented upon,
Have certainly done very well indeed.
The elder children bringing money in,
Father still working; with allowances
For this and that and little income-tax,
They probably earn seven times as much
As poor old Grosvenor-Smith. But who will grudge
Them this, their wild, spontaneous holiday?
The morning paddle, then the mystery tour
By motor-coach inland this afternoon.
For that old mother what a happy time!
At last past bearing children, she can sit
Reposeful on a crowded bit of beach.
A week of idleness, the salty winds
Play in her greying hair; the summer sun
Puts back her freckles so that Alfred Brown
Remembers courting days in Gospel Oak
And takes her to the Flannel Dance to-night.
But all the same they think the place 'Stuck up'
And Blackpool, next year – if there *is* a next.

SIR JOHN BETJEMAN
'Beside the Seaside', *Selected Poems*, 1948

PHILIP WILSON STEER
Southwold, 1889

I must go down to the seas again, to the lonely sea and the sky,
And all I ask is a tall ship and a star to steer her by;
And the wheel's kick and the wind's song and the white sail's shaking,
And a grey mist on the sea's face, and a grey dawn breaking.

I must go down to the seas again, for the call of the running tide
Is a wild call and a clear call that may not be denied;
And all I ask is a windy day with the white clouds flying,
And the flung spray and the blown spume, and the seagulls crying.

JOHN MASEFIELD
'Sea Fever', *Salt-Water Ballads*, 1902

SIR JOHN EVERETT MILLAIS
The North-West Passage, 1874

THE sea is the consolation of this our day, as it has been the consolation of the centuries. It is the companion and the receiver of men. It has moods for them to fill the storehouse of the mind, perils for trial, or even for an ending, and calms for the good emblem of death. There, on the sea, is a man nearest to his own making, and in communion with that from which he came, and to which he shall return. For the wise men of very long ago have said, and it is true, that out of the salt water all things came. The sea is the matrix of creation, and we have the memory of it in our blood.

There, sailing the sea, we play every part of life: control, direction, effort, fate; and there can we test ourselves and know our state. All that which concerns the sea is profound and final. The sea provides visions, darknesses, revelations. The sea puts ever before us those twin faces of reality: greatness and certitude; greatness stretched almost to the edge of infinity (greatness in extent, greatness in changes not to be numbered), and the certitude of a level remaining for ever and standing upon the deeps. The sea has taken me to itself whenever I sought it and has given me relief from men. It has rendered remote the cares and the wastes of the land; for of all creatures that move and breathe upon the earth we of mankind are the fullest of sorrow. But the sea shall comfort us, and perpetually show us new things and assure us. It is the common sacrament of this world.

HILAIRE BELLOC
The Cruise of the Nona, 1925

J M W TURNER
Peace: Burial at Sea, 1841

ACKNOWLEDGEMENTS

The publishers gratefully acknowledge permission to reproduce the following copyright material:

Hilaire Belloc,
extracts from *The Cruise of the Nona* (1925)
reprinted by permission of A. D. Peters & Co Ltd.

Sir Alan Herbert,
extract from *No Boats on the River* (1932)
reprinted by permission of Lady Herbert and Methuen London Ltd.

Cyril Ray,
extract from *Merry England* (1960)
reprinted by permission of Cyril Ray Esq.

Hammond Innes,
extract from *Harvest of Journeys*
reprinted by permission of Collins Publishers.

Frances Cornford,
'Summer Beach', *Travelling Home* (1948)
reprinted by permission of Century Hutchinson Limited.

Dylan Thomas,
extract from *Quite Early One Morning* (195-)
reprinted by permission of J. M. Dent & Sons Ltd and
David Higham Associates Limited.

John Betjeman,
extract from 'Beside the Seaside', *Collected Poems* (1948)
reprinted by permission of John Murray (Publishers) Ltd.

John Masefield,
extract from 'Sea Fever', *Salt-Water Ballads* (920)
reprinted by permission of The Society of Authors
as literary representatives of the Estate of John Masefield and
reprinted with permission of
Macmillan Publishing Company from *Poems*
by John Masefield (New York: Macmillan, 1953).

John Harris,
extract from 'The Land's End', *Songs from the Earth* (1978)
edited by D. M. Thomas reprinted by permission of Lodenek Press Ltd.

Raoul Dufy,
'Deauville, Drying the Sails' (1933)
© DACS 1986

André Derain,
'The Pool of London' (1906)
© ADAGP 1986

Oskar Kokoschka,
'Polperro II' (1939)
© ADAGP, Paris & COSMOPRESS, Geneve 1986